Way of the
Warrior

GLADIATORS
Battling in the Arena

Katherine Frew

HIGH
interest
books

Children's Press®
A Division of Scholastic Inc.
New York / Toronto / London / Auckland / Sydney
Mexico City / New Delhi / Hong Kong
Danbury, Connecticut

Book Design: Elana Davidian and Michael DeLisio
Contributing Editor: Geeta Sobha
Photo Credits: Cover, pp. 4, 16, 19, 29, 35, 39 © Bettmann/Corbis;
p. 7 © Christie's Images/Corbis; p. 8 © Patrick Ward/Corbis; p. 10 © The Huntington
Library, Art Collections, and Botanical Gardens, San Marino, California/SuperStock;
p. 12 © Private Collection/Bridgeman Art Library; p. 15 © Archives
Larousse/Giraudon/Bridgeman Art Library; p. 20 © Gian Berto Vanni/Corbis;
pp. 23, 26 © Stapleton Collection/Corbis; p. 30 © Louvre, Paris/Bridgeman Art
Library; p. 33 © Delaware Art Museum, Wilmington, DE/Bridgeman Art
Library/Samuel and Mary R. Bancroft Memorial; p. 36 © Araldo de Luca/Corbis;
p. 40 © Charles E. Rotkin/Corbis

Library of Congress Cataloging-in-Publication Data

Frew, Katherine.
   Gladiators : battling in the arena / Katherine Frew.
   p. cm. — (Way of the Warrior)
   Includes bibliographical references and index
   ISBN 0-516-25121-X (lib. bdg.) — ISBN 0-516-25090-6 (pbk.)
   1. Gladiators—Juvenile literature. I. Title. II. Series.

GV35.F74 2005
796.8'0937—dc22

                                                   2004003986

1 2 3 4 5 6 7 8 9 10 R 14 13 12 11 10 09 08 07 06 05

Contents

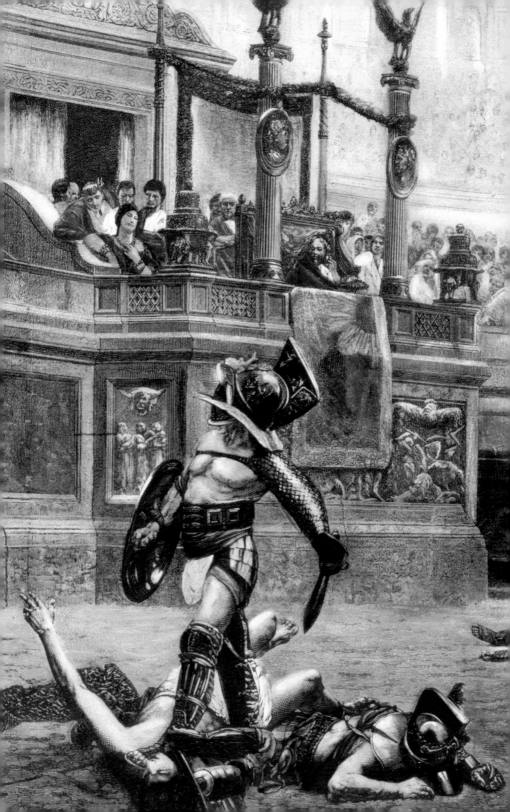

INTRODUCTION

It is a hot day in ancient Rome in the year A.D. 10. The Sun beats down on the sixty thousand people sitting in the bleachers of the Colosseum. This is Rome's largest outdoor arena.

The crowd cheers as two gladiators battle in the arena. The loud clang of swords rings in your ears. You are standing in a dark tunnel that leads to the arena's battlefield. Suddenly, the sound of clanging swords stops. Screams and cheers rise from the crowd. The cheers could only mean one thing. One of the gladiators has been killed. The crowd claps and cheers some more. The body of the fallen gladiator is removed from the field.

Your time has finally arrived. The door of the tunnel is opened and you walk into the arena. You are greeted by cheers from the crowd. You stand face-to-face with the warrior you will now battle. This is the same warrior who just killed a man. He stands behind a bloodstain that covers the ground.

Gladiators were Rome's celebrated warriors, fighting for their lives each time they entered the arena.

You raise your sword and shield and rush toward your opponent—knowing only one of you will survive this battle. You are a Roman gladiator.

Professional Warriors

Gladiator is a Latin word meaning "sword bearer." Gladiators were professional warriors who fought for the entertainment of the public. They had the skill, bravery, and popularity that we admire in professional athletes today. These professionally trained warriors were very popular and had many fans. But every time a gladiator entered the arena, he knew he would either die or have to kill whomever he was fighting!

Let's take a look at the bravery and skill involved in being one of these ancient warriors.

Before a fight, gladiators addressed the emperor with the phrase, "Those who are about to die salute you."

CHAPTER ONE

Let the Games Begin

Ancient Rome was a place of power and wealth. It was founded in 753 B.C. and was the capital city of the Republic of Rome, and later the Roman Empire. By the fourth century, the Roman Empire stretched from present-day England in the north to Turkey and Egypt in the south. One emperor ruled the people living in these lands.

Rome's favorite form of entertainment was the circus. The circus was the name given to an event that had many different games and races. There were chariot races, wild animals such as elephants and rhinoceroses fighting each other, and mock naval battles with real ships.

These are the remains of Hadrian's Wall in England. Many forts were built along this 73-mile (118 kilometers) wall. The forts kept invading tribes from Scotland out of Roman territory.

The most popular games, however, were the fights between gladiators, the celebrated warriors of Rome.

First Gladiators

Romans claimed that the people of ancient Etruria started gladiator games. Etruria was in the areas of Tuscany and Umbria in modern-day Italy. These gladiator fights were held to honor the dead.

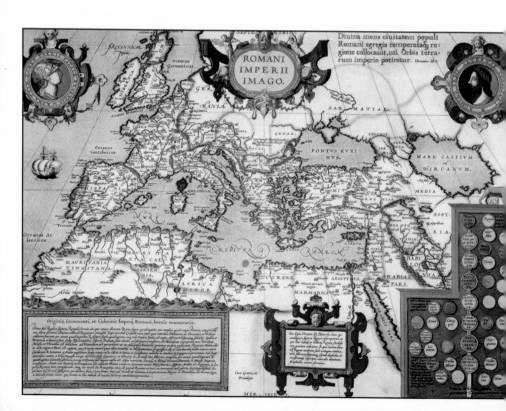

The first battle between gladiators in Rome took place in 264 B.C. Brothers Marcus and Decimus Brutus wanted to honor their father, Junius Brutus, at his funeral. Marcus and Decimus had three pairs of slaves battle each other in front of their guests. These gladiators fought to the death. The guests of Marcus and Decimus were highly entertained by the battles.

Gladiator fights became a major source of entertainment in Rome. In time, they were no longer held only at funerals. As these battles between gladiators became more popular, they became larger. By 183 B.C., games could involve up to sixty battles. In 65 B.C., 320 pairs of gladiators fought in a wooden amphitheater built by Roman general Julius Caesar. In A.D. 107, a celebration featured five thousand pairs of gladiators! Games were not just a useful way to entertain the public. They also served to show the military power and strength of Rome.

This sixteenth-century map shows the Roman Empire at its height. The Romans controlled all of Europe, northern Africa, and a large part of Asia.

11

Training a Gladiator

Gladiators were owned by *lanistae* who ran
training schools called *ludi*. Since they made
a living from renting out or selling gladiators,
lanistae were looked down on in Roman
society. Wealthy Romans, however, could own
gladiators without shame. They would hire a
lanista to train the gladiators.

The Circus Maximus in Rome was an arena used for chariot racing.
The track was wide enough for twelve chariots to race at the same
time. The arena could hold about 250,000 spectators.

A *lanista* rented his gladiators to whomever was having a circus. Gladiators were also used by politicians to control courts and the outcome of elections. At times, emperors used gladiators as bodyguards, hired killers, or even soldiers in wars. In A.D. 69, Emperor Otho used two thousand gladiators to strengthen his army. Marcus Aurelius, another emperor, formed an army of gladiators called the Obedient.

FIGHTING WORDS

Gladiator battles were called *munera*. The word means "duties." It refers to the duty of the living to the dead.

The Amphitheater

The ancient Roman amphitheater was designed to allow a large number of people to view the games. The creators of the amphitheater used a circular or oval design, with bleacher seats. They wanted the audience to surround the games. In fact, the word *amphitheater* is Greek, meaning "theater with seats on all sides." Many modern-day stadiums follow this ancient design.

The amphitheater had some very unique elements. For example, underneath the arena where battles took place was a network of underground passages. In these underground rooms and hallways, the gladiators waited for their turn to battle. This is also where animals, such as lions and bears, were kept. The animals fought people or other animals. For mock battles between ships, all the underground passages were flooded with water. The arena was filled with water so that real ships could sail and fight each other.

With such a variety of shows, it was very important to have large, well-built amphitheaters. The best example is the Flavian Amphitheater, also known as the Colosseum, in Rome, Italy. The Colosseum still stands today.

The Colosseum

The Colosseum was built between A.D. 70 and 80. It is 160 feet (49 meters) high. Originally, it spread across nearly 6 acres of land. It could seat about fifty thousand people. The Colosseum was built on a lake bed after all the water had been drained out. The builders put up walls around the hole and then made underground passages below the arena floor.

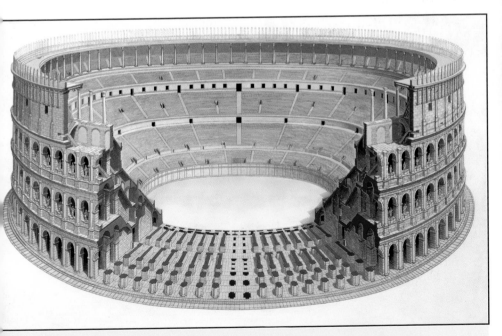

Marble was used for the seats of the Colosseum. Each seat was called a locus. Seating was assigned by a person's rank and class in society.

CHAPTER TWO

Gladiator Life

Gladiators came from all over the Roman Empire. They were people of many races and cultures, but most of them had one thing in common. They were not free. Almost all gladiators were criminals, slaves, or prisoners of war. They were forced to become gladiators. Free citizens could volunteer to become gladiators. A new gladiator was known as a *tiro*. A gladiator who fought well and lived through many games was called *primus palus*, or first sword.

This victorious gladiator is shown next to the body of his slain enemy. The gladiator holds a trident, which is a spear with three sharp prongs, and a net.

Criminals, Slaves, and Prisoners

There were two types of criminals who could find themselves fighting in a Roman amphitheater. The first was a criminal who had committed a capital crime, or a crime punishable by death. These criminals did not go to a *ludi* to become gladiators. These people were forced to fight without weapons and their death was certain. The second type was a criminal who had not committed a capital crime. This person might be made a gladiator. These people entered the *ludi* to learn gladiator fighting skills. Their punishment for the crimes they committed would be training and fighting for about five years.

Slaves who were strong and would make good fighters could be sold to a *lanista* for a lot of money. These slaves could earn their freedom if they were able to stay alive for the term of their service as gladiators.

Romans used slaves as more than gladiators. Slaves were also used as laborers and as symbols of their owners' ranking in Roman society.

Enemy soldiers captured by the Roman armies might also become gladiators. These prisoners of war were already trained to fight. They had a good chance of success against other gladiators they would battle in the arena.

The Volunteers

Free citizens who wanted to become gladiators gave up all rights of being a Roman citizen and were viewed as slaves. So why would anyone volunteer to become a slave? Some historians think that life as a gladiator might have actually been an improvement for many

At the *ludi*, gladiators trained on a central court such as this one in Pompeii, near present-day Naples, Italy. The gladiators' barracks surround the court.

free people. Life in the first century was difficult. Most people only lived until they were about twenty-five years old! Some people may have thought that taking their chances in the amphitheater wasn't such a bad deal.

Life in and out of the Arena

Although gladiators faced death each time they fought, they were treated well when they weren't fighting. Gladiators lived in barracks at the *ludi*. They were given three meals a day. Doctors were on hand if anyone got hurt during training. The gladiators were also treated if they got sick. These benefits were supplied to keep the warriors strong for combat.

Regardless of the benefits of housing, food, and medical attention, gladiators were not free. The barracks were like prisons. New gladiators were always guarded and

FIGHTING WORDS

The *ludi* began as training schools owned by one or two people. Eventually, the government took control of the training schools because it did not want anyone building a private army of well-trained fighters!

21

kept in shackles. Most gladiators did not like the cruelty of the games. Many even tried to commit suicide.

Gladiators fought about three or four times a year. If they were able to survive for five years, they could earn their freedom. A gladiator would have to face death and win about twenty times! Most never made it.

However, freedom was not the only reason that gladiators fought. A gladiator could earn fame and wealth. Gladiators who lived were paid after each fight. They could also earn a lot of money from their fans and the people who rented them. A gladiator who fought well could even become a hero in the eyes of the Romans. Imagine having thousands of people cheering you while you battle! If you win, they will adore you and scream in excitement. The possibility of this kind of fame even encouraged some emperors to take part in gladiator battles. For example, Emperor Commodus was said to have fought one thousand duels.

The emperor Commodus not only fought gladiators, but he hunted lions in the arena as well. Commodus used these fights to display his strength. He wanted the Roman people to view him as a god.

Fierce Females

There is evidence that women were also gladiators. It is not clear whether they were criminals, slaves, or volunteers. A large stone found by historians in Halicarnassus, in modern-day Turkey, shows a drawing of two women fighters. Their names are Amazonia and Achillea. They are shown without helmets and armed with swords. Historians think that women were as well trained as men and were armed with the same weapons. The famous Roman historian Juvenal wrote about women gladiators: *"Hear her grunt and groan as she works at it, parrying, thrusting; See her neck bent down under the weight of her helmet. Look at the rolls of bandage and tape, so her legs look like tree trunks."*

FIGHTING WORDS

Anyone who became a gladiator was immediately called *infamis*. This was a class of people who were not considered respectable. The word *infamis* eventually became our English word infamous, meaning to have a very bad reputation.

TOOLS OF THE TRADE

There were a variety of helmets, swords, and shields that gladiators used, and many different ways to fight. Some weapons the gladiators may have used include:

Galea: a helmet with a visor, or face protection, attached

Gladius: a gladiator's sword

Hasta: a lance used to spear the opponent

Iaculum: a net used by some gladiators

Manica: armor made of leather that covered a fighter's elbow or wrist

Parma: a round shield

Pilum: a spear used by Roman soldiers and some gladiators

Scutum: a large shield that was longer than it was wide

Emperor Septimius Severus at first allowed women to compete as gladiators, but banned the activity in A.D. 200. It's possible that the women gladiators had become so popular that even the rich, important women in society were interested in fighting.

CHAPTER THREE

A Warrior in Training

Gladiators lived by strict rules while training at the *ludi*. They had to follow a special diet. They exercised and trained in gymnastics regularly. They took lessons in how to use weapons from trainers who specialized in different weapons. To prevent injury during training, they used wooden swords in their lessons.

Types of Gladiators

There were different types of gladiators. The differences were based on the types of weapons that gladiators used. During their training, gladiators could choose the type of weapon and armor with which they wanted to

Gladiators were not just trained to fight well. They were also trained to kill their opponents quickly.

fight. This way the warriors fought with the weapons for which they were best suited. Most of the time, different types of gladiators were matched up against each other. Types of gladiators included the following:

Retiarius

The *retiarius* is sometimes called a "netman." This fighter was armed with a trident and a net. The *retiarius* used the net to keep his opponent at a distance. This fighter had to be quick and move around a lot in order to stay safe and to win.

Hoplomachus

The *hoplomachus* gladiator was well armed with a helmet, a round shield, and a complete suit of armor. The *hoplomachus* carried a short sword or dagger and a spear.

This painting shows a *secutor* (left) battling a *retiarius* (right). Though gladiators often fought in pairs, there were times when many gladiators would fight at the same time.

Secutor

The *secutor* used a sword and a shield. He wore a helmet and a *manica*. He usually fought against the *retiarius*.

Shown here is a bronze helmet that was worn by a *thraces* gladiator. *Thraces* style imitated fighters from Thrace, an ancient city.

Thraces

Thraces used a curved dagger and a small, round shield. He also wore a helmet and armor made of leather or metal on his legs. *Thraces* most often fought the *mirmillo* and the *hoplomachus*.

Mirmillo

The *mirmillo* wore a helmet, which had a fish on the crest, and body armor. He also wore a *manica*, an arm guard made of metal or leather. This gladiator carried a shield for protection.

Dimachaerius

The *dimachaerius* fought with two swords. Because this gladiator had no shield for protection, he would confuse his opponent by attacking with many quick blows. He probably wore body armor and a helmet as well.

Provocator

A *provocator* was armed with a shield, a short sword, and body armor. He wore a large helmet with flaps that covered the neck. His chest armor was large and sometimes even covered his shoulders. Unlike other gladiators, the *provocator* only fought other *provocators*.

Andabatae

The *andabatae* wore a helmet with a visor. During battle, they fought with the visor closed, and could not see well. Also, the *andabatae* fought on horseback.

Samnite

The *samnite* used a large, oblong shield and a short sword. His helmet had a large plume, or feather. On his left leg, he wore metal or leather armor.

Essedarri

The *essedarri* fought from chariots. Their fighting style was based on that of the ancient people of Britain.

Laquearii

The *laquearii* used a noose like a lasso to catch their opponents.

Animals were collected from all over the world to be part of the *venatio*.

Venatio

One game was called the *venatio*, meaning the hunt. Animals such as panthers, bears, wild goats, dogs, elephants, and camels were hunted. Most of these animals did not survive an encounter with an armed human fighter. Historians know that in some games as many as nine thousand animals were killed. Criminals who had committed capital crimes were made to fight the same kinds of wild animals *without* any weapons. These people were called *bestiarii* and were considered the lowest class of fighters at the games.

Finishing the Fight

Gladiators fought until one was defeated. When this happened, it did not always mean death, however. Sometimes the final decision was left to either the audience or the *editor*, the host of the games. Often the audience decided the fate of a defeated gladiator. If the defeated warrior put down his or her shield and lifted his or her left hand, the decision of death or mercy was in the hands of the audience. Sometimes people called out, *"Habet, hoc habet!"* which meant "He's had it!" and *"Mitte,"* or "Let him go!" Sometimes they called out, *"Iugula!"* which meant "Kill him!" The *editor* then made a final

The *editor* was the host of the games. Most of the time, this was the emperor himself. Shown here is Emperor Nero giving the sign that a defeated gladiator must die.

decision by gesturing with his hand. He would turn his thumb down or thrust his thumb at his heart to say that the gladiator should die. If the *editor* decided to grant the fighter mercy, he might wave a handkerchief or shout, "Dismissed!" While it was once believed that turning one's thumb up meant mercy, historians now understand that this is not true.

CHAPTER FOUR

Fighting to the End

The fact that the games lasted for over five hundred years is proof of their popularity among Romans. There are many theories about why Roman people enjoyed battles to the death between two human beings so much. One theory is that ancient Romans thought that dying bravely was very important. However, not every Roman was impressed by the gladiator fights. Emperors such as Augustus Caesar and Marcus Aurelius tried to limit the number of games held.

Marcus Aurelius ordered the gladiators of his time to fight with blunted swords. When he died, his son Commodus became emperor of the Roman Empire.

Spartacus

The legends of some gladiators are still alive today. The feats of Spartacus prove that not all gladiators accepted their fates as a part of the circuses. Spartacus was a hero to Roman slaves. He is one of the most famous gladiators of all time. He is not famous for his battles in the amphitheater, but for his battle for freedom outside of it.

Spartacus was not happy being a slave and being forced to fight for the entertainment of the Roman people. In 73 B.C., he led a group of gladiators to form a small army and flee to Mount Vesuvius, in southern Italy. They defeated many Roman soldiers. However, Spartacus was eventually killed in a battle with Marcus Licinius Crassus, a Roman officer. Thousands of Spartacus's followers were killed. When Spartacus's camp was invaded, the Roman army found about three thousand Roman prisoners who were unharmed.

The series of battles led by Spartacus is known as the Gladiators' War. It began at the *ludi* in Capua. At its height, Spartacus's army grew to about ninety thousand people.

Fall From Glory

There are many factors that led to the end of the games. The circuses were becoming very costly to run. Also, many lives were being lost in these violent contests. The rise of the Christian religion also affected the end of the games. Emperor Constantine, who ruled from

A.D. 323 to 337, outlawed the gladiator games in 325, but they continued anyway. Constantine declared Christianity the new religion of Rome in 337. Before this, many Christians were being thrown into the arenas because their religious beliefs were different from those of most Romans. After 337, Christians could speak out against the games.

One famous legend of how the games truly ended involves Saint Telemachus, a Christian. Telemachus was from Asia. In his travels, he visited Rome. There, he saw a battle between two gladiators. He went into the ring to try to stop these men from killing each other. Unfortunately, the audience didn't like Telemachus ending their fun. They were so angry that they stoned Telemachus to death. When Emperor Honorius heard of Telemachus's death, he declared a true end to all battles between gladiators.

The final decision was made and gladiators were officially out of a job in 405. The world was changing and the Roman Empire was no longer as strong. After the games ended, the world would never again witness a form of entertainment that was so brutal. The gladiators and the Roman Empire became a chapter in history. But a gladiator's life of courage and his survival skills continue to fascinate people to this day.

Today, the Colosseum still stands in the city of Rome, Italy. In 2000, the Greek National Theater put on a series of plays there. These were the first shows at the Colosseum in fifteen hundred years.

New Words

amphitheater (**am**-fi-thee-uh-tur) a large, open-air building with rows of seats in a high circle around an arena

arena (uh-**ree**-nuh) a large area that is used for sports or entertainment

barracks (**ba**-ruhks) the building or buildings where soldiers live

bleachers (**blee**-churz) raised seats or benches arranged in rows

capital crimes (kap-**uh**-tuhl **krimz**) crimes for which the criminal is punished by death

chariot (**cha**-ree-uht) a small vehicle pulled by a horse, used in ancient times in battles or for racing

Christianity (kriss-chee-**an**-uh-tee) the religion based on the life and teachings of Jesus Christ

combat (**kom**-bat) fighting between people or armies

New Words

gymnastics (jim-**nass**-tiks) physical exercises that involve difficult and carefully controlled body movements

historian (hi-**stor**-ee-uhn) a person who studies and writes about history

mock (**mok**) false or imitation, as in mock battle

naval (**nay**-vuhl) to do with a navy or warships

opponent (uh-**poh**-nuhnt) someone who is against you in a fight, a contest, an election, or a debate

outlawed (**out**-lawd) to have forbidden something by law

Roman Empire (**roh**-muhn **em**-pire) the system of government that was the strongest in the world from about 27 B.C. to A.D. 476; the capital was Rome

trident (**trye**-dent) a type of spear with three prongs

visor (**vye**-zur) the movable, see-through shield on the front of a helmet that protects the face

43

For Further Reading

Ganeri, Anita. *Emperors and Gladiators.*
New York: McGraw-Hill Children's Publishing,
2001.

Mannix, Daniel P. *The Way of the Gladiator.*
New York: ibooks, Incorporated, 2001.

Marks, Anthony, and Graham Tingay.
The Romans. Tulsa, OK: EDC Publishing, 1990.

Nardo, Don. *Life of a Roman Gladiator.*
Farmington Hills, MI: Lucent Books, 2003.

Resources

Web Sites

Classics Technology Center:
The Roman Gladiator
*http://ablemedia.com/ctcweb/consortium/
    gladiator1.html*
Check out this Web site to learn about gladiators
and ancient Roman sports and culture.

Roman Gladiators
*www.fortunecity.com/underworld/straif/69/
    enggladiat.htm*
This Web site provides information on the lives
of gladiators as well as their fighting methods.

UNRV History: Roman Gladiator Types
www.unrv.com/culture/roman-gladiators.php
This Web site provides descriptions of the
different kinds of gladiators.

Resources

History for Kids! Ancient Rome
www.historyforkids.org/learn/romans/index.html
Learn more about the ancient Roman civilization. This Web site includes information on language, religion, clothes, and more.

You Wouldn't Want to Be a Roman Gladiator!
http://www.salariya.com/web_books/gladiator/ index.html
This fun Web site takes you through the life of a gladiator. Place your cursor over the images to see the author's take on how gladiators may have felt about their fate.

Index

Index

About the Author

Katherine Frew is a writer living in Texas, where she is currently working on her master's degree in English literature.